CONTEMPORARY'S

CHOICES
AN ESL LIFESKILLS SERIES FOR ADULTS
IT'S YOUR RIGHT

JOHN CHAPMAN

Project Editors
Julie Landau
Charlotte Ullman

Consultants
Aliza Becker
ESL Consultant
Chicago, Illinois

Diego Bonesatti
Technical Adviser
Chicago, Illinois

Terence J. Bray
Hacienda La Puente
Unified School District
Hacienda Heights, California

CB
CONTEMPORARY
BOOKS
CHICAGO

Library of Congress Cataloging-in-Publication Data

Chapman, John, 1944–
    It's your right / John Chapman.
        p.   cm.—(Choices: an ESL lifeskills series)
    Includes index.
    ISBN 0-8092-4043-2 (paper)
        1. English language—Textbooks for foreign speakers.   2. Law—
United States—Problems, exercises, etc.   3. Life skills—Problems,
exercises, etc.   4. Readers—Life skills.   5. Readers—Law.
    I. Title.   II. Series: Choices (Chicago, Ill.)
    PE1128.C527   1991
    428.2'421—dc20   91-35083
                                                                                              CIP

Choices: An ESL Lifeskills Series for Adults was developed
for Contemporary Books by **Quest Editorial Development,
Inc.** Sylvia Bloch, editor.

Published by Contemporary Books, Inc.
180 North Michigan Avenue, Chicago, Illinois 60601
Manufactured in the United States of America
International Standard Book Number: 0-8092-4043-2

Published simultaneously in Canada by
Fitzhenry & Whiteside
91 Granton Drive
Richmond Hill, Ontario L4B 2N5
Canada

Editorial Director
Caren Van Slyke

Editorial
Betsy Rubin
Marietta Urban
Claudia Allen
Janice Bryant
Lisa Dillman
Esther Johns

Editorial Production Manager
Norma Fioretti

Cover Photograph © C. C. Cain

Production Editor
Jean Farley Brown

Cover Design
Lois Stein

Illustrator
Gary Undercuffler

Art & Production
Jan Geist

Typography
Terrence Alan Stone

■ ■ ■ ■ ■ Contents

■■■■■ To the Student

Welcome to *It's Your Right*!

It's Your Right is part of Contemporary's *Choices: An ESL Lifeskills Series for Adults*.

This book will give you information about laws in the United States and about your legal rights and responsibilities. *It's Your Right* will also give you the language skills you need to use that information.

You may already know about the laws in your native country. *It's Your Right* encourages you to compare the way you do things in your native country with the way you do things in the United States.

It's Your Right offers valuable information about:

- getting a driver's license
- reporting an accident
- getting married
- registering to vote
- voting and getting involved in politics
- free speech
- reporting crime
- rights of the accused
- taxes
- discrimination in employment
- immigration and U.S. citizenship

and other rights and responsibilities.

We hope you enjoy *It's Your Right*.

■ ■ ■ ■ ■ To the Teacher

Level

Choices: An ESL Lifeskills Series for Adults is designed for ESL students who are at the intermediate level. **Choices** will guide students in making informed decisions about their lives in the U.S., based on the knowledge they bring from their native countries. **Choices** will help students acquire the lifeskills competencies, language skills, and cultural information they need to make effective choices in the U.S.

Rationale

It's Your Right provides a student-centered approach to language learning. It offers detailed information about rights and responsibilities in the U.S. while providing opportunities for cultural comparison and teaching practical language skills. The **Choices** series features natural language that adult students can put to immediate use in their daily lives.

Format

It's Your Right contains a *Tips for Teachers* section, twelve chapters, four review units, an appendix, and an index. The review units are interactive information-gap exercises that appear after every three chapters, incorporating content from those chapters. The authors acknowledge Judith Winn-Bell Olsen and Richard C. Yorkey as sources of inspiration in these exercises.

> For step-by-step information on how to use this book and for additional classroom activities, see **Choices Teacher's Guide** 2.

Tips for Teachers

Everyone from the beginning teacher to the experienced professional can benefit from teaching suggestions. What follow are notes on the purpose of the sections in *It's Your Right* and how to use them.

The **Before You Listen** section prepares students for the dialogue by encouraging them to discuss the picture that illustrates it. Ask students to predict what they think will happen in the dialogue. This is a good time for you to assess how much the students know about the topic. If you want to emphasize key words before students listen to the dialogue, consult the **Words to Know** section.

There are a number of ways to present the **Dialogue**. It is helpful to act out the dialogue, doing something to indicate that you are portraying different people talking. For example, you may want to use different voices or change positions as you change roles. If the resources are available, you may wish to record the dialogue ahead of time. If you do this, make sure each character is vocally distinct, so that students know who is talking.

Discuss the dialogue, using the **Talking It Over** questions as a guide. Ask students if they have had experiences similar to the situation in the dialogue.

Assign different groups of students to different roles corresponding to the characters in the dialogue. Have them repeat their roles after you. Have students practice the dialogue in pairs or groups. Ask for volunteers to perform the dialogue for the class. Many of the dialogues are open-ended. Have students invent their own endings.

Words to Know presents vocabulary that students need to know to understand the dialogue. The blank lines allow students to personalize the text by adding their own words to the vocabulary list. Encourage students to guess the meaning of vocabulary through the context and to refer back to the picture.

Another Way to Say It offers alternatives for some of the idiomatic expressions that are introduced in the dialogue. Have students read the dialogue again, inserting the new expressions. The blank lines allow students to personalize the text by adding their own words to the vocabulary list.

Talking It Over should foster discussion about the situation presented in the dialogue and invite students to talk about how their own experiences relate to the situation. The questions in this section range from simple comprehension to application of the information to students' lives.

In **Working Together**, a role-play activity, students create conversations and put to use the language they have just learned. You may want to write the sample conversation on the board and ask students what they think should come next. Write their ideas on the board. After students have written the conversation as a class, have them practice it in pairs or groups and ask for volunteers to role-play it for the class. Then, have students create individual conversations based on relevant experiences.

Real Talk shows students how speakers of American English really talk. For that reason, it's important to use natural pronunciation when you present this section.

Putting It Together presents grammar in context. It focuses on one useful structure that appears in the dialogue. There is a short presentation of the structure and then a contextual exercise. This is followed by the opportunity to use the structure in meaningful, real-life responses.

In the **Read and Think** sections, students are asked to guess the meanings of underlined words. The content reading on this page provides information that students can put to use immediately. The **Read and Think** page is a reading passage of an example of the kinds of reading materials that people have to deal with every day, such as campaign literature, graphs and charts, paycheck stubs, yellow pages ads, and government forms.

In Your Community offers students an opportunity to explore the community resources available to them. They can do this individually or in pairs or groups. You may also want to take students to a community-based organization during class time, invite a speaker to the classroom, or bring in realia such as actual examples of the items mentioned above.

Figuring Out the U.S. features an intimate look at one aspect of U.S. culture. Students are encouraged to circle any words in the passage they don't understand and to try to guess their meanings from the context.

Your Turn gives the students a chance to compare life here with life in their native countries and opens up avenues to a variety of choices. Depending on the proficiency level of your students, the writing activity may range from a simple list to a paragraph or more expressing an opinion.

1 I Plan to Drive to Work

Before You Listen

1. What does the Motor Vehicle Bureau do?
2. What are the people waiting for?
3. Did you drive in your native country? Did you need a driver's license?
4. Do you need a driver's license to drive in the U.S.? What do you know about getting a driver's license in the U.S.?

■■■■■■ I Plan to Drive to Work

Listen carefully to the dialogue.

Carol: Is this the first time you've taken a road test?

Bounpho: Yes, it is. I drove for ten years in Laos, and now I have to prove that I know how to drive.

Carol: That's too bad. I'm really nervous. I passed the written test the first time I took it. But I failed the road test.

Bounpho: Was it hard?

Carol: Not really. I did well on things like stopping, starting, and parallel parking. But I forgot one turn signal.

Bounpho: Orahan, how many times can you take the road test?

Orahan: They give you four chances, Bounpho.

Carol: Yeah, but if you mess up four times, you have to wait a year to try again.

Orahan: You know, I messed up on my first road test. But the next time, I passed. I'm sure you'll both do fine today.

Carol: I hope so. I need a license so I can drive my friends to the mall.

Bounpho: And I'm getting a job. I plan to drive to work every day.

Orahan: Oh, here comes the examiner. Good luck, you two.

Words to Know

Motor Vehicle Bureau	written test	turn signal
road test	failed	license
passed	parallel parking	examiner
	_____	_____

Another Way to Say It

That's too bad. .... I feel sorry for you.

mess up .... do poorly; make mistakes

do fine .... succeed

_____ .... _____

■■■■■ Talking It Over

Discuss the questions in pairs or in groups.

1. Has Carol taken the road test before?
2. What part did she have trouble with?
3. Did Bounpho drive in Laos?
4. What does Carol want to do when she gets her license?
5. Do you think Carol will pass this time? Why or why not?
6. How do you think Bounpho will do on her road test? Why?
7. In your native country, do most people have cars? Do you need a driver's license? How do you get one?
8. Have you taken a driver's test in the U.S. or in your native country? What was the test like? What was the hardest part? the easiest?
9. What kinds of problems can you have if you drive without a license in the U.S.?

Working Together

Work with your classmates and teacher to finish this conversation. Imagine that you want to get a driver's license and you are talking with a clerk at the Motor Vehicle Bureau.

You: What do I have to do to get a driver's license?

Clerk: First you have to take a written test.

Real Talk

You *have to* wait a year to try again.

People in the United States often say "hafta" in informal conversation. However, it is always written *have to*.

■■■■■ Putting It Together

> **Have to/Can**
> *Have to* means that you must do something. It is required.
> *Can* means that it is possible, but not necessary, to do something.
>   I **have to** prove that I know how to drive.
>   I **can** drive my friends to the mall.

Practice A

Complete the following sentences using *have to* and *can*.

Orahan's friend: What do I do to get a driver's license?

Orahan: First you ___*have to*___ get a permit so you can practice driving with a licensed driver.

Orahan's friend: Who should I get to teach me how to drive?

Orahan: You _____ go to a driving school.

Orahan's friend: _____ I ask my friends to teach me instead?

Orahan: Yes, you _____. But they _____ have driver's licenses and be over 18 years old.

Orahan's friend: _____ you go with me to get my permit now?

Orahan: No. I _____ go to work. But I

_____ go with you tomorrow afternoon.

Orahan's friend: Great! I'll meet you here at two o'clock.

Practice B

List some of the things you *have to* do to get a driver's license in your native country. Then list some things you *can* do after you get a license. Share your answers with the class.

    Example: *In Laos you have to take an eye exam to get a driver's license.*

■ ■ ■ ■ ■ Read and Think

As you read this advertisement, underline the words you don't understand and discuss them with the class. Then answer the questions.

ACE DRIVING SCHOOL
Call 555-7767

- New cars with dual controls
- Written test and road test preparation
- Free door-to-door service
- Days, evenings, weekends
- Standard and automatic transmissions
- Nervous students our specialty
- Cars available for road test
- Graduates guaranteed lower insurance rates

1. What are some of the services offered by Ace Driving School?
2. How is the practice car different from a regular car? Why?
3. Why do you think insurance companies give lower rates to people who complete a driver's training course?
4. Do you know anyone who has attended a driver's education course? What does he or she say about the classes?

In Your Community

Find out the information individually or in groups and share it with your class.

1. How much does it cost to take a course at a driving school? What languages do the instructors speak? How much time do they spend with each student?
2. Are driver's education classes offered at high schools or community colleges in your community? How much do they cost? What are the hours?
3. Where is the nearest Motor Vehicle Bureau? What hours is it open?
4. What proof of age and identity is required to apply for a driver's license? (birth certificate? alien registration card? other?)
5. What tests do you have to take to get a driver's license?
6. How much does it cost to get a license?

■ ■ ■ ■ ■ Figuring Out the U.S.

As you read the passage, circle any words you don't understand and try to guess their meanings.

Taking Your Road Test

When you take a road test, you have to supply your own car. Many driving schools will let you use one of theirs, or you may borrow one from a friend. Before you can take the test, however, the car you bring in must pass some tests of its own.

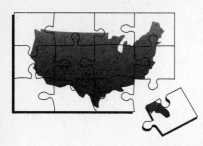

The inspector will check to see that the car has an up-to-date inspection sticker. The headlights, taillights, and turn signals must all be working. The steering and brakes have to work well. The tires must not be worn down, and mirrors and windows cannot be cracked or broken. Some states check to see that the car is not giving off dangerous fumes from the exhaust system.

In addition to checking on the condition of the car, the inspector will ask you to show the vehicle registration and the insurance papers. Unless you have all these items, you will not be allowed to take the road test in that car. It is a good idea to locate all the required documents a couple of weeks before your test. That way you can spend the last few days preparing yourself for the driving test, instead of preparing the car.

Your Turn

Discuss the questions.

1. Why do you think your car must be in good condition for the road test?
2. Why do states require cars to pass a yearly inspection? Is there a car inspection system in your native country? If so, what do the inspectors check for?
3. How important is it for you to have a driver's license? How would your life be different without one?

Choose one of the questions and write about it.

Before You Listen

1. What has happened to the parked car?
2. What do you think caused the accident?
3. Have you ever seen an accident like this? What did the driver do?

▪▪▪▪▪ At Least No One Got Hurt

Listen carefully to the dialogue.

Fernando: Are you OK, Tony?

Tony: Yeah, I'm fine. What about you?

Fernando: I'm not hurt. I was worried about that little boy on the bicycle. I guess I was watching him instead of looking where I was going.

Tony: Well, at least no one got hurt. What are you going to do now?

Fernando: I guess I should try to find the owner. He's going to be angry. It looks like a new car.

Tony: That's true. But he probably has insurance that will take care of most of the damage. Are you going to call the police?

Fernando: Do you think I should? I don't want to have a bad driving record.

Tony: Well, the law says you're supposed to call the police. But no one saw the accident. You could just forget it. You pay to have your car fixed up and let that guy's insurance company pay for his repairs.

Fernando: I could probably get away with it. But I don't know if it's the right thing to do.

Words to Know

hurt	insurance	police
at least	damage	repairs
owner	_____	_____

Another Way to Say It

take care of .... pay for

fixed up .... repaired

get away with it .... escape without being caught

_____ .... _____

■■■■■ Talking It Over

Discuss the questions in pairs or in groups.

1. Why did Fernando have the accident?
2. Was anyone hurt in the accident?
3. Why doesn't Fernando look for the owner right away?
4. Why doesn't Fernando call the police immediately?
5. Do you think Fernando will find the owner and call the police? Why or why not?
6. What might happen to Fernando if he doesn't report the accident?
7. Do you know anyone who has been in an accident like this? What did that person do? Why?

Working Together

Work with your classmates to finish the conversation below. Then practice with a partner.

Sally: I just hit a parked car. Thank goodness nobody got hurt!

Leona: Are you going to find the owner and report it to the police?

Real Talk

I don't *want to* have a bad driving record.

People in the United States often say "wanna" in informal conversation. However, it is always written *want to*.

> ## Could/Should
>
> *Could* is used to show that an action is possible. *Should* shows that an action is a good idea.
>
>   Examples: I **should** try to find the owner.
>   You **could** just forget it.

Practice A

Complete the following sentences using *could* and *should*.

Sally: I just had a minor car accident. ___*Should*___ I leave a note for the owner of the other car?

Leona: Well, I think you _____, but you _____ get into trouble.

Sally: What _____ happen to me?

Leona: The other person might call the police. They _____ ask you a lot of questions.

Sally: _____ I tell them what really happened?

Leona: I think that's the best idea. Otherwise, you _____ get into more trouble.

Sally: Well, now I know what I _____ do, but I wish I _____ do something else.

Practice B

Now imagine that Sally was in a more serious accident. She was driving home after a party, and she was drunk. She went through a stoplight and hit another car. What should Sally do? What could happen? Discuss your answers in small groups.

■■■■■ Read and Think

Work in pairs. Imagine that two cars have hit each other on a busy street and you need to fill out an Accident Report form for your insurance company. Decide on names, addresses, and other information.

What to Do in Case of an Accident

Accident Report

Date _____ Hour _____ Location _____

Vehicles Involved
Vehicle No. 1 (yours)

License Plate No. _____ State _____ Make _____ Model _____

Type (sedan, truck, etc.) _____ Color _____

Owner's Name and Address _____

_____ Tel. No. _____

Driver's Name _____ Address _____

_____ Driver's Lic. No. _____

Vehicle No. 2
Owner's Name and Address _____

Driver's Name and Address _____

Tel. No. _____ Driver's Lic. No. _____

License Plate No. _____ State _____ Make _____ Model _____

Witnesses (including police)

Name _____ Address _____

Name _____ Address _____

In Your Community

Find out the information individually or in groups and share it with your class.

1. Collect more information on how to report an auto accident in your community. Bring in your state driver's manual, insurance company pamphlets, and driver's training textbooks. In small groups, discuss what you should do in case of an accident.
2. Contact your local police department and arrange for an officer to come in and talk about auto safety and what to do in case of an accident.

■ ■ ■ ■ ■ Figuring Out the U.S.

As you read the passage, circle any words you don't understand and try to guess their meanings.

Some Rules of the Road

The following rules of the road may vary from state to state.

- You must pull over to the right and stop when an ambulance, fire truck, or police car approaches you from behind with the siren going.
- In your car, you can take only the number of people for whom you have seat belts. Also, children under 40 pounds or 4 years must be in a car seat at all times.
- It is illegal to throw anything out of a car window. You may have to pay a fine of up to $500 for littering.
- It is illegal to drink alcohol and drive. People who drink and drive may lose their licenses and can even go to jail.

Some U.S. Customs

- On national holidays, many people drive with their lights on during the day to remind everyone to drive extra carefully.
- It is very impolite to interrupt a line of cars going to a funeral. A funeral procession moves very slowly, and the cars have their headlights on.

Your Turn

Discuss the questions.

1. Are you surprised by any of the rules and customs listed above? Which ones? Why?
2. List some driving rules and customs in your native country that are different from those in the U.S.
3. Do you think that the way some people drive shows you something about their personalities? Give examples.

> *Choose one of the questions and write about it.*

3 | Something Old, Something New

Before You Listen

1. What kind of store are the women in?
2. What do you think they are talking about?
3. What does Carol think about the price of the dress?

■■■■■ Something Old, Something New

Listen carefully to the dialogue.

Esin: Thanks for coming to help me choose a wedding dress.

Carol: That's OK, Esin. It's kind of fun. But getting married seems pretty expensive.

Esin: It sure is! I know that the bride's parents usually pay for the wedding, but I think Jim and I should foot the bill.

Carol: Good for you! Are you going to take Jim's last name?

Esin: Of course. I have to, don't I?

Carol: No, you can keep your maiden name if you want. I know a lot of women who have.

Esin: Really? Well, I'm sure Jim would like me to take his name. But I'll think about it first.

Carol: Sure. And will you go on a honeymoon?

Esin: Oh yes. We're going to go to the mountains for a week. Carol, can I ask you something? Someone told me we need to wear something blue at the wedding. Why is that?

Carol: Well, the groom doesn't need to wear anything blue. But there's a tradition that the bride wears something old, something new, something borrowed, and something blue. I think it's for good luck.

Esin: Look at this price tag! I guess my good luck hasn't started yet.

Words to Know

wedding	maiden name	tradition
married	honeymoon	borrowed
bride	groom	
_____	_____	_____

Another Way to Say It

foot the bill .... pay for it

I guess .... It seems true

_____ .... _____

■■■■■ Talking It Over

Discuss the questions in pairs or in groups.

1. What is Esin buying?
2. Who is going to pay for the dress?
3. Why do you think Esin feels that she and Jim should pay for their own wedding?
4. Do you think Esin is going to change her last name when she gets married? Why or why not?
5. Who pays for the wedding in your native country?
6. In your native country, does the woman change her last name? How? Does the man change his last name?
7. What are some wedding traditions in your native country?

Working Together

Esin and Jim are discussing their wedding. Work with a partner to finish the conversation.

Esin: I think we should pay for our own wedding.

Jim: Well, I'm not so sure. What's wrong with asking your parents to pay?

Real Talk

People in the United States often say "gonna" in informal conversation. However, it is always written as *going to*. Look at the following example.

You may say: We're "gonna" go to the mountains.

But always write: We're *going to* go to the mountains.

Future with _Going To_

Going to plus a verb describes an action that is planned for the future. _Going to_ is often used in place of _will_.

Jim and I are **going to** foot the bill.

Are you **going to** take Jim's last name?

Practice A

Answer the following questions using _going to_ plus a verb.

1. Will Esin get married soon?

   Yes, she's _going to get married_ very soon.

2. Will her parents pay for the wedding?

   No, they're not _____ for the wedding.

3. Will they invite a lot of people to the wedding?

   Yes, they're _____ about 50 people.

4. Will they go on a honeymoon?

   Yes, they're _____ to the mountains.

5. Will Esin wear something new at the wedding?

   Yes, she's _____ the new wedding dress.

6. Will Esin buy the expensive dress?

   No, she probably isn't _____ it.

Practice B

Work in small groups. Practice asking each other questions about your future plans. The person asking the question uses _will_, and the person who answers uses _going to_.

Person A: Will you change jobs soon?

Person B: No, I'm going to keep this job.

OR: Yes, I'm going to quit next week.

■■■■■ Read and Think

Read the passage and try to guess the meanings of the underlined words.
Then answer the questions.

Marriage Laws in the U.S.

In the United States, each state has its own set of rules and <u>regulations</u> about marriage. You can go to your local city hall to find out how to apply for a marriage license.

In most states, a man and woman must be over 18 years old to marry without <u>parental consent</u>. In some states, you must be at least 22 years old. All states require <u>proof of identity</u>. Some states require <u>blood tests</u>. These tests check for <u>sexually transmitted diseases</u>. In states where blood tests are required, you must apply for the license soon after the tests are finished—usually within 30 days. In addition, some states require a <u>physical examination</u>.

State laws do not allow <u>close relatives</u>, such as brothers, sisters, and first cousins, to marry each other. If a person was married before, he or she must show that the first marriage was ended <u>legally</u>, such as by divorce. A person who marries again without ending the first marriage is <u>guilty</u> of <u>bigamy</u>, which is <u>illegal</u>. Most states require a waiting period between applying for the marriage license and getting married. This gives the couple time to be sure they want to marry.

1. Where do you apply for a marriage license?
2. What kinds of tests might you have to get a marriage license?
3. What are some reasons a couple would not be allowed to get married?
4. Why do most states require a waiting period between getting the marriage license and getting married?
5. Do you have any friends who were married in the U.S.? What have they told you about the process?
6. Do you think it is good to have so many regulations governing marriage? Why or why not? Why do you think these regulations exist?

In Your Community

Find out the information individually or in groups and share it with your class.

1. Where can you apply for a marriage license in your town?
2. What proof of identity must you show? What tests do you need?
3. How long do you have to wait between getting the license and getting married?
4. What is the minimum age to get married in your state?

As you read the letters, circle any words you don't understand and try to guess their meanings.

Alice Advises
No More Old-Fashioned Marriage . . . or Divorce

Dear Alice: I have been married for six years. Both my husband and I work full-time. But he expects me to do all the housework and to let him decide how we spend our money. I say we should share the work and decision making, but he says that men shouldn't do "women's work" and that men know more about money. What do you say?

—A Worn-Out Wife

Dear Worn-Out: I say you know what you are talking about. You obviously know how to earn money, and you have a right to decide how it's spent. And when both partners work outside the home, they had better both work inside the home too. Are you any less tired than he is at the end of the day? Also, many men end up feeling good about sharing the decision making and helping with housework and child care. It makes them feel closer to the family and often leads to a happier home life.

Dear Alice: My marriage is a mess! Lately my wife and I have been disagreeing about everything. And the fighting is starting to affect the children. We can't seem to talk to each other anymore. I don't want to think about divorce, but it's beginning to seem like the only way. Can you help?

—Confused

Dear Confused: The first thing to do is get some outside help. Set up a meeting with a religious adviser, or a professional marriage counselor.

If your problems are too big and you decide to divorce, get legal advice right away. If you agree to separate, you can save a lot of money through a "no-fault" divorce. You will have to decide together on child support, child custody, and the division of your possessions. It might make you feel a little better to realize that you are not alone—today about half of marriages in the U.S. end in divorce. Good luck!

Your Turn

Discuss the questions.

1. Why do you think some men feel they should not be responsible for housework and child care?
2. Do you agree with Alice's advice to "Worn-Out"? Why or why not?
3. How are marriages in the U.S. different from those in your native country? Which do you prefer? Why?
4. Is divorce legal in your native country? Do many people get divorced?
5. Why do you think the divorce rate is over 50 percent in the U.S.?

Choose one of the questions and write about it.

■■■■■ Review Unit One

Person A

Age of First Marriage

Below is a chart that shows the average age of first marriage in the U.S. Some parts are missing. Your partner has the information you need. Get the missing information by asking questions. Your partner will look at page 20. Do not look at your partner's page.

All information in this section is about people over 18 years old, living in the United States. All numbers are approximate. Add the missing information to the chart. Then discuss the questions together.

Age of First Marriage*		
Year	Men	Women
1960	_____	21
1970	_____	21
1980	25	_____
1989	26	_____

1. What are some advantages of early marriage?
2. What are some advantages of later marriage?
3. Do you think it's important to get married?

Marriage and Divorce

Here is a chart showing the number of marriages and divorces in the U.S. between 1960 and 1990. Some parts are blank. All numbers are approximate. Get the missing information from your partner without looking at his or her page. Then discuss the questions that follow.

Marriage and Divorce*		
Year	Marriages	Divorces
1960	1,500,000	_____
1970	_____	800,000
1980	2,500,000	_____
1990	_____	1,200,000

1. How did the number of marriages per year change between 1960 and 1990?
2. What happened to the number of divorces per year during the same period?
3. What do you think caused these changes?

———————

*The U.S. Department of Labor *Monthly Labor Review,* March 1990

Person B

Age of First Marriage

Below is a chart that shows the average age of first marriage in the U.S. Some parts are missing. Your partner has the information you need. Get the missing information by asking questions. Your partner will look at page 19. Do not look at your partner's page.

All information in this section is about people over 18 years old, living in the United States. All numbers are approximate. Add the missing information to the chart. Then discuss the questions together.

Age of First Marriage*		
Year	Men	Women
1960	23	———
1970	23	———
1980	———	22
1989	———	24

1. What are some advantages of early marriage?
2. What are some advantages of later marriage?
3. Do you think it's important to get married?

Marriage and Divorce

Here is a chart showing the number of marriages and divorces in the U.S. between 1960 and 1990. Some parts are blank. All numbers are approximate. Get the missing information from your partner without looking at his or her page. Then discuss the questions that follow.

Marriage and Divorce*		
Year	Marriages	Divorces
1960	———	500,000
1970	2,200,000	———
1980	———	1,200,000
1990	2,500,000	———

1. How did the number of marriages per year change between 1960 and 1990?
2. What happened to the number of divorces per year during the same period?
3. What do you think caused these changes?

---

*The U.S. Department of Labor *Monthly Labor Review*, March 1990

Before You Listen

1. Why is Joe Howard talking to people in front of the supermarket?
2. What do you think Bounpho is asking?
3. Have you ever talked to someone from your city or town government? What questions did you ask?

■■■■■ Elect Joe Howard

Listen carefully to the dialogue.

Joe: Hi! I'm Joe Howard. I'm running for councilman in the 16th District. I hope you'll vote for me in next week's election.

Bounpho: Can I ask you some questions? The sign says you want safer streets. What do you plan to do?

Joe: For one thing, I am asking for more streetlights to make the streets brighter at night. I'm also working to have more police assigned to the neighborhood.

Bounpho: That sounds good. I have a child, and I worry sometimes.

Joe: Does your child go to the George Washington School?

Bounpho: Yes. She's in the third grade.

Joe: Well, another thing I'm working on is smaller class sizes at that school. There are more than 30 children in some classes!

Bounpho: I know. It's important to have smaller classes. But we also really need a recreation center for teenagers. If we don't give them a safe place to meet, they'll end up joining gangs.

Joe: You're right. I can't promise a recreation center this year, but I'll work on it. Please remember to vote. Nice meeting you.

Bounpho: Nice to talk with you. Good-bye.

Words to Know

councilman	election	recreation center
district	assigned	gangs
vote for	neighborhood	promise
_____	_____	_____

Another Way to Say It

I'm running for	I'm a candidate for
That sounds good.	That seems like a good idea.
I'll work on it.	I'll try to make it happen.
_____	_____

■■■■■ Talking It Over

Discuss the questions in pairs or in groups.

1. What does Joe plan to do to make the streets safer?
2. What does he want to do to improve the schools?
3. What does Bounpho ask him to work on?
4. What does Joe want Bounpho to do?
5. Do you think Bounpho will vote for Joe? Why or why not?
6. Can you believe all the promises a candidate makes? Why or why not? How can you find out what that person has already accomplished?
7. Are there elections in your native country? If not, how are leaders chosen?

Working Together

Before you talk to someone who is running for the city council, you have to think about what you want. Work with a partner to list several things that would improve your neighborhood. Then write a conversation with your partner. Person A wants to be elected. Person B is asking for improvements in the neighborhood.

Person A: I am working for better schools for our district.

Person B: Good. And we need a recreation center for teenagers, too.

Real Talk

In informal conversation, we often leave out the beginning of a sentence. Joe says "Nice meeting you" instead of "It was nice meeting you." Listen as your teacher reads the examples that follow. What's missing?

Nice to talk with you.

See you later.

Too bad!

Can you think of any other examples?

■ ■ ■ ■ ■ **Putting It Together**

> **Comparisons with -er**
> One way to make comparisons is to add -er to short adjectives (words that describe people, places, or things).
>   Streetlights make the streets **brighter**.
> If an adjective ends in y, change the y to i and add -er.
>   New trees will make the streets **prettier**.

Practice A

Answer these questions using adjectives with -er or -ier.

1. Why will the city add more streetlights?

    It will make the streets ___safer___. (safe)

2. Why does Bounpho want a recreation center in the neighborhood?

    It will keep the young people _____. (busy)

3. Why will the school hire four new teachers?

    It will make each class _____. (small)

4. What is a change that everyone wants in his or her district?

    They want to make the neighborhood _____. (clean)

5. What will happen if people clean up the streets?

    It will make the neighborhood children _____. (healthy)

Practice B

Work with a partner. Write about some changes you'd like to see in your neighborhood. Make comparisons by adding -er or -ier to some of these adjectives: *smooth, safe, clean, healthy, bright, large, pretty, new.*

   Example: *We need smoother sidewalks.*

■■■■■ Read and Think

Read the passage and try to guess the meanings of any words you don't know. Then answer the questions.

The Three Levels of Government in the U.S.

LOCAL (CITY)

Head: mayor or city manager

Some important functions:
- makes and enforces laws about traffic and parking, building construction, and garbage disposal
- may be responsible for a fire department and a police force
- issues marriage licenses

STATE

Head: governor

Some important functions:
- is responsible for its own school system, police force, and health department
- issues driver's licenses
- provides aid to unemployed persons

FEDERAL

Head: president

Some important functions:
- defends the country through the army, navy, and other armed forces
- controls trade among the states
- controls trade between the U.S. and other countries
- prints money
- regulates immigration and naturalization
- provides aid to poor people and senior citizens

---

1. What are the three levels of government in the U.S.?
2. Who heads each level of government?
3. Each level of government has different responsibilities. Give some examples for each level.
4. What are the levels of government in your native country?
5. How is the government there different from the government here?

In Your Community

Find out the information individually or in groups and share it with your class.

Learn more about your city or town government. Who is the mayor or city manager? Who is your councilman or councilwoman? Where are the city offices located? What services does your city offer its residents?

People who want you to vote for them often use political brochures like the one below. Read it carefully and circle any words you don't understand.

**ELECT JOE HOWARD
COUNCILMAN
16TH DISTRICT**

Joe Howard and his family have lived in the 16th District for 11 years. Mrs. Howard is the principal of George Washington School, and the Howards' children attend local public schools.

Joe Howard promises you:

SAFER STREETS
He helped start a community watch program on his block. And you'll find him patrolling the street with his neighbors once a week. Joe Howard will fight to get more police assigned to high-crime areas.

BETTER SCHOOLS
As a teacher, and then head of the teachers' union, he supported the purchase of more computers and the expansion of computer training programs in elementary and high schools. As your councilman, he'll work to reduce class sizes in the schools.

LESS GANG VIOLENCE
Joe Howard helped organize after-school activities for teenagers. More than 200 young people regularly attend these sports and music programs. Joe is committed to keeping kids off the streets and stopping gang violence.

**JOE HOWARD WILL FIGHT FOR THE RIGHTS OF
THE 16TH DISTRICT.
HE'LL WORK FOR YOU!**

• **VOTE FOR JOE HOWARD** •

Your Turn

Discuss the questions.

1. What does the brochure tell you about Joe Howard? What kind of information is missing?
2. Why does the brochure have a picture of Joe Howard's wife and children? Do they help make him a strong candidate? Why or why not?
3. Do candidates use brochures like this in your native country? How are campaign materials different there?

Choose one of the questions and write about it.

Have You Registered to Vote Yet?

Before You Listen

1. What do you think the League of Women Voters is?
2. What are these two people talking about?
3. Have you ever voted in an election?
4. What do you know about voting in the United States?

■ ■ ■ ■ ■ Have You Registered to Vote Yet?

Listen carefully to the dialogue.

Luz: Hello, Mr. Colón. We're having a voter registration drive. Have you registered to vote yet?

Fernando: No. It's too much trouble. There are too many things to fill out on the form.

Luz: But it only takes a few minutes.

Fernando: Thanks, but I don't think my one vote really makes any difference.

Luz: You're right. Most of the time, a single vote doesn't matter that much. But your vote along with other people's votes can make a big difference.

Fernando: Well, maybe. But I don't think elections are honest. Sometimes, people vote more than once. Sometimes, votes are thrown away.

Luz: Yes, that does happen at some polling places. But there are laws about elections. People can and do report vote fraud, and the government usually takes action. Your vote could help elect a candidate you believe in, you know.

Fernando: Maybe you're right.

Luz: So, can I send you a voter registration form?

Fernando: Well . . .

Words to Know

voter registration drive	single	polling places
form	honest	vote fraud
	_____	_____

Another Way to Say It

too much trouble .... very difficult to do

makes any difference .... has an effect

takes action .... does something about the problem

_____ .... _____

■ ■ ■ ■ ■ Talking It Over

Discuss the questions in pairs or in groups.

1. Who is calling Fernando? Why?
2. What is a voter registration drive?
3. Why hasn't Fernando registered to vote yet?
4. How does he feel about voting?
5. Do you think he will register and vote?
6. Do you think Fernando is a citizen? Why or why not?
7. Did you vote in your native country? Why or why not? Did you have to register?

Working Together

Many people in the United States never register or vote. Work with a partner to list reasons why some people don't vote and several reasons why they should vote. Then write a conversation between one person who never votes and another person who thinks it's important to vote.

Person A: I don't vote because it's too much trouble to register.

Person B: It's not so hard. And don't you want to help elect people you trust?

Real Talk

The words *to* and *too* sound the same when we pronounce them alone. However, they sound different when we pronounce them in a sentence. In a sentence, *to* sounds like "tuh" and *too* sounds like the number "two." Listen to your teacher say these sentences:

He isn't registered *to* vote. He says it's *too* much trouble.

Too much/Too many

We use the phrases *too much* and *too many* when there is more of something than we want. *Too much* is used with things you can't count. *Too many* is used with things you can count.

I'm not going to register to vote. It's **too much** trouble.

There are **too many** things to fill out on the form.

Practice A

Complete the following dialogue with a partner using the phrases *too much* and *too many*.

Carol: Are you going to vote tomorrow, Dad?

Carol's dad: No. It takes _too____ _much___ time. Besides, those

councilmen all make _____ _____ promises. "Safer streets! Better schools!"

Carol: But we need to change some things about our neighborhood, don't we?

Carol's dad: No. I think we've had _____ _____ changes already.

And they all cost _____ _____ money.

Carol: But we have to do something.

Carol's dad: I know what I'm doing. I'm going back to the office. I've got

_____ _____ work to do.

Practice B

Work with a partner. Write five sentences using *too much* and *too many*. You can use the words below to get started if you want.

questions money repairs time work

■■■■■ Read and Think

Read the form and try to guess the meanings of any words you don't know. Fill out as much of the form as you can. Then answer the questions. Note: If you are a permanent or undocumented resident, pretend you are a citizen as you do this practice exercise.

Voter Registration Application
1. Name of applicant (please print)

   Last _____ First _____ Middle _____

2. Street Address _____

   City or Town _____ County _____ Zip Code _____ Phone ( )

3. This form is being used as ( ) new registration   ( ) change of address

   (date moved) _____

4. Birth Date   Month _____ Day _____ Year _____

5. From what address did you last register to vote? Under what name?

   Last _____ First _____ Middle _____

   Street Address _____

   City or Town _____ County _____ State _____ Zip Code _____

6. I am a ( ) native born ( ) naturalized citizen.

   I was naturalized   Month _____ Day _____ Year _____

7. A. By the time of the next election, I will be 18 years of age.
   B. I will be a citizen of the U.S. and will have lived in this state and county for 30 days.
   C. To the best of my knowledge, the above statements made by me are true and correct.
   D. I understand that any false or fraudulent registration may subject me to a fine of up to $1,000, imprisonment up to five years, or both.

   Signature of Applicant   Date of Signature

   _____   _____

---

1. What voting requirements are listed in sections 7A and 7B of the Voter Registration Application?
2. What is the purpose of sections 7C and 7D? Why do they ask you to sign the form?
3. Have you ever registered to vote? Was the application difficult to fill out?

In Your Community

Find out the information individually or in groups and share it with your class.

Where do you go to register to vote? Can you register by mail? When is the next election in your community? Who is being elected, or what is being voted on? Do you plan to vote in this country? Do you think voting can make a difference in the future of your neighborhood?

■■■■■ Figuring Out the U.S.

As you read the passage, circle any words you don't understand and try to guess their meanings.

The Two-Party System

Most people in the United States belong to one of two political parties—the Republicans or the Democrats. Recent Republican presidents include George Bush, Ronald Reagan, and Richard Nixon. Former Democratic presidents include Jimmy Carter and John F. Kennedy.

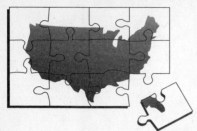

It is hard to describe the differences between the present Republican and Democratic parties in a few words. And in some recent election years, it has become very difficult to tell the parties apart. However, the following lists will help you understand some of the traditional differences.

Republicans	Democrats
• believe the state should decide how many benefits to give its residents	• believe federal government should guarantee all U.S. citizens certain benefits
• believe big businesses should pay low taxes so they have money to create jobs	• believe big businesses should pay high taxes because they make a lot of money
• believe poor people will work harder without government help	• believe in programs to help poor people

Your Turn

Discuss the questions.

1. What are some basic differences between the Republicans and the Democrats? Do you agree with the ideas of either party?
2. In your native country, are there several political parties? What are they? How are they different from each other?
3. Is it important to have more than one political party? Why or why not?

Choose one of the questions and write about it.

Before You Listen

1. Where are these people?
2. Why are they carrying signs? What do the signs mean?
3. What do you think the two people in front are talking about?
4. Have you ever seen anything like this? Where?

■ ■ ■ ■ ■ We Have the Right to Free Speech

Listen carefully to the dialogue.

Al: What is this all about, Luz?

Luz: A woman was mugged in the elevator last week. We're angry about the lack of security in our building.

Al: I can understand that. But couldn't you just talk to the people at Burton Management?

Luz: We've been telling them we need security guards for months! They couldn't care less.

Al: But do you have to have a demonstration? I live in the neighborhood, and all the noise and cars stopping really bother me.

Luz: I know it bugs you, but we have the right to free speech. What Burton Management is doing is wrong. We have to make them do something about the situation!

Al: But sometimes these things get out of hand. People get hurt.

Luz: Someone already *has* gotten hurt. The woman who was mugged is in the hospital right now.

Al: That's terrible, but there must be some way to get action without demonstrating.

Luz: Look at it this way. If you don't support other people's right to free speech, that right may not be there when you need it.

Al: I hadn't thought of it that way before.

Words to Know

mugged	management	free speech
elevator	security guards	situation
lack	demonstration	support
_____	_____	_____

Another Way to Say It

couldn't care less .... aren't concerned at all

it bugs you .... it bothers you

out of hand .... out of control

_____ .... _____

▪▪▪▪▪ Talking It Over

Discuss the questions in pairs or in groups.

1. What is happening in front of the apartment building?
2. Why is Al upset?
3. What does Al think the tenants should do instead?
4. What does Luz say about free speech?
5. Do you think Al has ever been in a demonstration? Why or why not?
6. Do you think it is possible to have free speech without ever bothering other people? Explain.
7. Are there ever demonstrations in your native country? If so, describe one.

Working Together

Work with your classmates and teacher to finish the conversation below. Imagine that you are watching a demonstration with a friend. Talk about what you see happening and what you think about it.

You: What are all those people doing?

Your friend: I'm not sure. I think they want better security in their building.

Real Talk

In conversation, people often say "couldn't cha." However, it is always written *couldn't you*. Listen as your teacher reads this sentence:

But *couldn't you* just talk to the people at Burton Management?

> ### *Have/Has* + *Already* + *Past Participle*
> *Have* or *has* + *already* + the past participle of a verb shows that something has happened before a certain time.
>
> Someone **has already gotten** hurt.
>
> I **have already reported** the problem.
>
> **Note:** The past participles of most verbs end in *-ed*. Common irregular past participles are listed on pages 83 and 84 of this book.

Practice A

Respond to each sentence using *have* or *has* + *already* + past participle.

1. Let's *complain* to the people at Burton Management.

   We _have already complained_ to them.

2. Someone should *speak* to the building manager.

   Luz _____ to her.

3. Let's *report* the problem to the newspaper.

   We _____ the problem.

4. Someone should *tell* the management we need security guards.

   We _____ them we need guards.

5. I think the demonstration will *start* soon.

   The demonstration _____.

6. I think the police will *get* here soon.

   Look! Two police officers _____ here.

Practice B

Work with a partner to write sentences using *have/has* + *already* + past participle. Write about things that you have already done today, this week, this month, or this year.

Example: I *have already paid* my phone bill.

■■■■■ Read and Think

Read these letters to the editor from the local newspaper. Try to guess the meanings of the underlined words. Then answer the questions.

Dear Editor:

I think it's about time our city government took legal action against Burton Management. There have been three fires in Burton buildings in the last month. In one building, two people got hurt when the fire escape collapsed. In another building, there were no smoke alarms, and fire broke out while people were sleeping. It was lucky no one was killed. Do we have to wait for someone to die before the fire inspectors start doing their job?

The laws are on the books. The city should enforce them.

LUCY JAFFE
Upland

Dear Editor:

I am writing in support of Denise Buyer for councilwoman in the 16th District. She has lived in the district longer than her opponent, Joe Howard, and she understands the needs of the people better. She'll help lower our taxes. We already spend enough money on the schools, but Mr. Howard wants to spend more. He would make our taxes go up, not down. And Ms. Buyer will work harder for us. When you vote next week, think about who can do the job best and vote for Denise Buyer.

GERALDO DIAZ
Upland

1. What is Ms. Jaffe angry about? Who does she feel is responsible?
2. What does Ms. Jaffe think should be done about the problem? Do you agree? Why or why not?
3. Why does Mr. Díaz think Denise Buyer is the best candidate for the job?
4. Why does he think people should not vote for Joe Howard?
5. In the U.S., newspapers often print letters from people who criticize the government or political candidates. Do you think it's good for the newspapers to print these letters? Why or why not?

In Your Community

Work in small groups.

Each group will choose a neighborhood problem and write a letter to a newspaper, a councilman/councilwoman, or a business owner about it. When the letters are finished, share them with the class.

■ ■ ■ ■ ■ Figuring Out the U.S.

As you read this dialogue, circle any words you don't understand and try to guess their meanings.

Block Associations

Orahan, Bounpho, and Fernando are waiting for the bus at the corner of the street they live on.

Fernando: Doesn't it bother you that there's so much trash in the street?

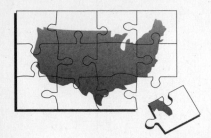

Bounpho: Yeah, my children are always getting cut on pieces of broken glass. You would think the city would come and clean it up.

Orahan: Well, I've complained to our councilman many times. He always says he'll take care of it right away.

Fernando: I think we have to get together to change things ourselves.

Orahan: Maybe we need to form a block association.

Fernando: Do you think we could call a meeting next week? We could put up signs and talk to our neighbors so a lot of people would come.

Bounpho: What would we talk about?

Orahan: The same things we always complain about. Dirty streets. Gangs.

Fernando: We could come up with ways we can improve things ourselves and also figure out how to get the city to help us.

Bounpho: Maybe we could meet in the church at the corner. Shall we ask the minister tonight?

Fernando: Why not?

Your Turn

Discuss the questions.

1. Why do you think the city doesn't keep the streets cleaner?
2. What are some things about your neighborhood that need to be improved? Is anyone in the neighborhood working to make them better? How?
3. In your native country, do people work together to change things? Can they get the government to make changes? How?

> *Choose one of the questions and write about it.*

Person A

Work with a partner. One of you should look only at this page, and the other should look only at page 40. Take turns asking each other for a definition of each word that is not filled in on your puzzle. At the end, go over all answers with your partner.

The first answer is written in for you. All answers are from Chapters 1–6. Some are two words long.

Example: Person A: What is number 1 down?
Person B: It's a group of people marching and carrying signs.

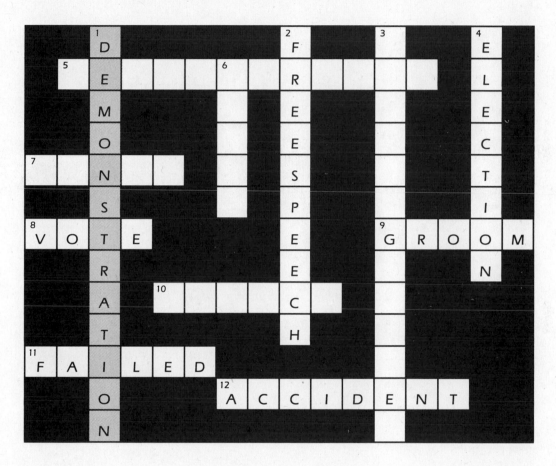

Person B

Work with a partner. One of you should look only at this page, and the other should look only at page 39. Take turns asking each other for a definition of each word that is not filled in on your puzzle. At the end, go over all answers with your partner.

The first answer is written in for you. All answers are from Chapters 1–6. Some are two words long.

Example: Person A: What is number 1 down?

Person B: It's a group of people marching and carrying signs.

Before You Listen

1. What happened to the first-floor window?
2. Why does Esin look so worried?
3. Who do you think she is talking to on the phone?
4. Has something like this ever happened to you?

■■■■■ We'll Send Someone Right Away

Listen carefully to the dialogue.

Operator: Emergency, Operator 17.

Esin: Hello. Hello. I think someone is breaking into an apartment across the street. And I'm uhh . . .

Operator: What's the address of the apartment?

Esin: It's 613 Dennis Street, near Lucas Avenue.

Operator: Did you say 630 or 613?

Esin: Six thirteen. Six-one-three.

Operator: OK. Now tell me what happened.

Esin: I heard a crash and looked outside. I saw a man climbing into a broken window on the first floor. I couldn't see him clearly, so I can't give you a description.

Operator: That's OK. Will you leave your name and number?

Esin: Umm . . . OK. I'm Esin Aslan, and my number—

Operator: Slow down. How do you spell that?

Esin: E-S-I-N. A-S-L-A-N. And my number is 555-8976. Please send someone right away!

Operator: OK, miss. We're sending someone right now. Stay where you are.

Esin: Don't worry. I will.

Words to Know

emergency	address	crash
operator	_____	_____

Another Way to Say It

breaking into	....	forcing their way into
Slow down.	....	Speak more slowly.
right away	....	immediately; right now
Don't worry.	....	You can be sure of it.
_____	....	_____

■■■■■ Talking It Over

Discuss the questions in pairs or in groups.

1. Who is Esin calling? Why? What number do you think she called?
2. What information does the operator ask for?
3. How is Esin feeling? How can you tell?
4. Why does the operator ask Esin for the address of the apartment before asking what has happened?
5. Esin gives her name and phone number. Do you think she has to do this?
6. Why does the operator tell her to stay where she is?
7. Do you think she will leave her apartment before the police arrive? Why or why not?
8. Have you ever reported a crime? If so, describe what happened.
9. Name some other crimes you might need to report.

Working Together

Imagine that your car has been stolen. Work with your classmates to finish this conversation.

Operator: Emergency, Operator 22.

You: This is [your name]. I'm calling to report a stolen car.

Real Talk

THIRty	thirTEEN	SEVenty	sevenTEEN
FORty	fourTEEN	EIGHty	eighTEEN
FIFty	fifTEEN	NINEty	nineTEEN
SIXty	sixTEEN		

It is often difficult to hear the difference between numbers like *thirty* and *thirteen*. One way to make it clearer is to stress the first or last syllable (part of the word) as this list shows.

Commands and Polite Requests

In an emergency, people often give each other commands. In normal situations, we use a polite request (with *please* or *can*) and a softer tone of voice. With your teacher, listen to and repeat the following examples. Notice the different tone of voice as well as the different words.

Commands	Polite Requests
Wait a minute.	Wait a minute, **please**.
Tell me what happened.	**Can** you tell me what happened?
Stay where you are.	**Please** stay where you are.

Practice A

Label the following sentences *C* for commands and *P* for polite requests.

1. _____ Come here.

2. _____ Don't move.

3. _____ Can you tell me your address?

4. _____ Slow down.

5. _____ Can you wait here?

6. _____ Sit here, please.

Practice B

Go over the answers to Practice A with the teacher. Then work in pairs. Write down a situation in which each sentence in Practice A could be used correctly. Review your answers with the teacher.

1. _A mother is telling a child to get away from a big dog_.

2. _____.

3. _____.

4. _____.

5. _____.

6. _____.

▪▪▪▪▪ Read and Think

Read the police handout and try to guess the meanings of the underlined words. Then answer the questions.

If You've Been Robbed . . .

You come home from work at 7:00 and find that your door <u>lock</u> is broken and the door is open. You've been robbed!

DON'T go inside. The <u>intruder</u> may still be in your home.

DO call the police and wait for them to arrive before entering your home.

DON'T touch anything. The police will look for <u>clues</u>, and you could <u>destroy</u> them.

To help the officer:

DO give the police all important details you can think of.

DO make a list of each missing item. Write a <u>description</u> including <u>brand name</u>, size, color, and price.

DO ask neighbors if they saw or heard anything <u>unusual</u>.

To prevent another robbery:

DO <u>install</u> strong locks on windows and doors.

DO leave a light on if you go out during the evening.

---

1. What should you do if your home is robbed? What shouldn't you do?
2. How can you help the police do their job?
3. Name two ways to prevent robberies.

In Your Community

Find out the information individually or in groups and share it with your class.

What is the telephone number of the police precinct closest to your house? What is the street address? Do the police have translators? What languages do they speak? Is there another number to call in case of an emergency? (911?)

▪▪▪▪▪ Figuring Out the U.S.

As you read the passage, circle any words you don't understand and try to guess their meanings.

Forming a Block Watch Group

Orahan, Bounpho, and Fernando are setting up chairs for the block association meeting at the church.

Bounpho: Do you think this group can do anything about all the robberies in our neighborhood?

Fernando: I don't know, but my brother was robbed last week, and he didn't even report it. He figures he'd never get his television back anyway.

Orahan: That's terrible. I know some people who were robbed too. They're pretty sure they know who did it. But they didn't call the police, because they're afraid that the guy's family might do something to hurt them.

Bounpho: I think it's terrible when people are afraid to report a crime. Someone I know was mugged and lost fifty dollars. But he doesn't have a green card, so he didn't go to the police.

Fernando: Well, we have to do something . . . Maybe we could form our own block watch group and walk up and down the block in pairs every night, watching out for people who might steal cars or rob houses. We can call the police if we see anything unusual.

Bounpho: Does it make a difference?

Fernando: There are usually fewer muggings and stolen cars after people start a block watch group.

Orahan: Well, maybe we should try it.

Your Turn

Discuss the questions.

1. What are some reasons people do not report robberies to the police? Do you feel the same way? Why or why not?
2. Do you think neighborhood organizations like this block watch group can make a difference? Would you join one? Why or why not?
3. In your native country, is crime a problem? What kinds of crime? Do neighbors look out for each other? What do people do to prevent crime?

Choose one of the questions and write about it.

---

8 | He Didn't Do It!

Before You Listen

1. Where are these people? What's happening?
2. Why do you think the police are questioning the man?
3. What do you think Esin is thinking?
4. Have you ever seen something like this? Describe the situation.

■■■■■ He Didn't Do It!

Listen carefully to the dialogue.

Levent: I don't get it! Why do you want to take me to the police station?

Det. Connor: A man was mugged around the corner on King Street at twelve thirty. The guy knocked him down and took his wallet.

Levent: But why do you think *I* did it? I was just visiting my sister at her job.

Det. Connor: The mugger was about your age and height, and he was wearing dark pants and sunglasses.

Esin: Officer, my brother didn't do it. He's been with me since twelve o'clock. We were just coming back from lunch.

Levent: Yeah. It must be somebody else.

Det. Connor: Well, I have to ask you to come in for questioning anyway. If you won't cooperate, I'll have to arrest you.

Esin: You can't arrest him. He didn't do it!

Words to Know

police station	height	cooperate
detective (Det.)	sunglasses	arrest
wallet	officer	_____
_____	_____	

Another Way to Say It

I don't get it! .... I don't understand!
knocked him down .... pushed him to the ground
_____ .... _____

▪▪▪▪▪ Talking It Over

Discuss the questions in pairs or in groups.

1. What happened to the man on King Street? When did it happen?
2. Why do the police think Levent did it? Do you think the police have a good description of the suspect? Why or why not?
3. Where has Levent been since twelve o'clock?
4. How is Levent feeling? How is Esin feeling?
5. Should Levent request a lawyer before answering the questions?
6. Have you ever seen the police arrest anyone? What happened?
7. What would you do if something like this happened to you?

Working Together

Work with your classmates and teacher to finish the conversation that follows. Imagine that an apartment has been robbed and that the police want to take you to the police station for questioning. You want to explain that you didn't do it.

Police officer: You'll have to come with me.

You: Why do I have to go to the police station?

Real Talk

When you ask a *wh*-question (using *who, what, where, when,* or *why*), your voice drops at the end of the question.

Example: *But why do you think I did it?*

When you ask a yes/no question, your voice rises at the end.

Example: *Do you know Esin?*

Listen to your teacher ask several questions of each type. Then make up some questions of your own and practice with a partner.

> ### *Ago/Since*
>
> *Ago* is used with a period of time (for example, two hours) to show how far in the past something happened. The simple past tense is used with *ago*. *Since* is used with clock time (such as 2:00) to show how long something has been happening. The present perfect tense is used with *since*.
>
> He **left** home two hours **ago**.
>
> He's **been** with me **since** 12:00.

Practice A

Pretend that it is now 1:00. Look at the clocks in the pictures above and fill in the blanks.

1. Esin has been at work since ___8:00___ this morning.

2. She arrived at work _____ ago.

3. Esin and Levent went to lunch _____ ago.

4. They have been gone since _____.

5. Detective Connor learned about the mugging _____ ago.

6. Detective Connor has been looking for the mugger since _____.

Practice B

Work with a partner to write sentences using *since* and *ago*. Write about things that have happened to you today.

Examples: *I came to school two hours ago.*
I haven't eaten since 8:00.

Read the passage and try to guess the meanings of the underlined words. Then answer the questions.

The Rights of the Accused

Before 1966, many people who were arrested did not know their rights. Now, if a person is <u>accused</u> of <u>committing</u> a crime, the police must follow certain rules.

The police must tell the <u>suspect</u> his or her rights and be sure the suspect understands them. The police must read the list of rights in the person's native language, if necessary. After an arrest, the suspect can make one phone call. The suspect also has the right to talk to a lawyer, or <u>attorney</u>, before answering any questions.

All suspects are considered <u>innocent</u> until proven <u>guilty</u>. The court makes the final decision about whether a suspect is guilty or innocent of a particular crime.

The *Miranda* Warning

In 1966, the United States <u>Supreme Court</u> ruled that the police must tell people their rights when they are arrested. The statement of rights is called the *Miranda* warning.

"You have the right to <u>remain silent</u>. Anything you say can and will be used against you in court. You have the right to have a lawyer present during questioning. If you cannot <u>afford</u> a lawyer, one will be <u>appointed</u> for you, and you will not be questioned until your attorney is present. Do you understand these rights?"

The exact wording of the *Miranda* warning is not the same in all parts of the country.

---

1. Is a person accused of a crime considered innocent or guilty? Do you think this is a good idea? Why or why not?
2. What are some of the rights guaranteed by the *Miranda* decision?
3. If you were arrested, would you want to remain silent? Why would you need a lawyer present during questioning?
4. Compare your rights in the U.S. with those of a person accused of a crime in your native country. How different are they?

In Your Community

Find out the information individually or in groups and share it with your class.

What legal help is available in your community? Contact the American Civil Liberties Union, a legal aid society, and religious organizations. Bring back any brochures or other printed information that is available.

Study the drawing and read the passage. Circle any words you don't understand and try to guess their meanings.

Trial by Jury

If a person is accused of a crime, he or she has the right to a trial. At the beginning of most trials, the prosecuting attorney and defense attorney tell what they think the evidence shows. The prosecuting attorney speaks for the plaintiff (the person who is making the complaint). The defense attorney

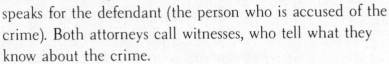

speaks for the defendant (the person who is accused of the crime). Both attorneys call witnesses, who tell what they know about the crime.

The judge supervises the trial from a large desk called the *bench*. The jury (usually 12 people) listens to everything that is said. Finally, the two attorneys give closing statements, and the judge gives final instructions to

the jury. The members of the jury then go to another room to decide whether the defendant is guilty or not guilty. Later, they return to the courtroom and tell the judge their decision. If the person is found guilty, the judge will determine the sentence.

Your Turn

Discuss the questions.

1. Describe how a courtroom is set up.
2. What does the prosecuting attorney do? the defense attorney? What do witnesses do?
3. What are some of the things the judge does during a trial?
4. Do you think that the jury system guarantees a fair trial? Why or why not?
5. Is the court system in your native country the same as in the U.S.? Explain the differences.

> *Choose one of the questions and write about it.*

I Just Got My First Paycheck

Before You Listen

1. Where are Luz and Bounpho?
2. What kind of work does Luz do?
3. What is Bounpho holding in her hand?
4. What do you think she is asking Luz?

■■■■■ I Just Got My First Paycheck

Listen carefully to the dialogue.

Bounpho Phoumy	077-
Gross Pay	350.00
Fed. Inc. Tax	70.00
S. S. Tax	21.00
State Inc. Tax	3.00
MEDC	18.00
Savings Plan	20.00
Net Pay	218.00

Luz: Hi, Bounpho. What's up?

Bounpho: Hi, Luz. I just got my first paycheck.

Luz: That must feel great! And how do you like your job?

Bounpho: The job's fine, but I have some questions about my paycheck.

Luz: Oh? What's the matter? Maybe I can help.

Bounpho: Look how much they took out for taxes! The government gets almost as much as I do.

Luz: Well, it's not that bad. And when you file your income tax return in April, you'll be glad you paid the money now.

Bounpho: Why do you say that?

Luz: Well, the company usually deducts enough taxes during the year so that you don't have to pay anything in April. You may even get a refund.

Bounpho: But they take out money for a lot of other things too. What's this $18.00 for MEDC?

Luz: That's your part of the medical insurance payment. Sometimes a company will pay for all of it, but you usually have to pick up a percentage yourself.

Bounpho: They're taking out more than $100 of my pay every week. Isn't there some way I can change that?

Words to Know

personnel	file	refund
paycheck	income tax return	medical insurance
taxes	deduct	payment
_____	_____	percentage

Another Way to Say It

That must feel great! .... You must be happy!

pick up .... pay

_____ ....

■■■■■■ Talking It Over

Discuss the questions in pairs or in groups.

1. What has Bounpho just received?
2. Why is she happy? Why is she unhappy?
3. Why is she talking to Luz about her paycheck?
4. What will Bounpho have to do in April?
5. Will Luz have to do the same thing? Why?
6. How do you think Luz feels about paying taxes? Why?
7. If you work, how many deductions are there on your paycheck? What are they for?
8. How do you feel about all these deductions? Are there any you think you should not have to pay?
9. Do people pay income tax in your native country? Compare the system there with the one in the U.S.

Working Together

Work with your classmates and teacher to finish this conversation. Imagine that Bounpho and her mother are preparing dinner and discussing Bounpho's first paycheck.

Bounpho: I got my first paycheck today, but they took out more than $100.

Bounpho's mother: One hundred dollars! Why?

Real Talk

There are informal ways to ask how someone is feeling and to find out what is wrong. When Luz asks Bounpho *What's up?*, she wants to know how Bounpho is. When Luz asks *What's the matter?*, she is asking Bounpho to tell her what the problem is.

Work with a partner. Come up with situations when you would say *What's up?* and *What's the matter?*

> **Sometimes and Usually**
>
> These words show how often something happens.
>
> How Often?
>
> *Sometimes* 10–50 percent of the time
>
> *Usually* 50–80 percent of the time
>
> **Sometimes** a company will pay for all of it, but you **usually** have to pick up a percentage yourself.

Practice A

Work with a partner. Rewrite the following sentences using *sometimes* or *usually*.

1. I get a paycheck almost every Friday.

   I usually get a paycheck _____ on Friday.

2. Some Fridays I go straight to the bank after work.

   _____ after work on Friday.

3. I earn more than $300 most weeks.

   _____ more than $300 per week.

4. I earn more than $400 a few weeks of the year.

   _____ more than $400 per week.

5. They almost always take out over $100 in taxes.

   _____ over $100 in taxes.

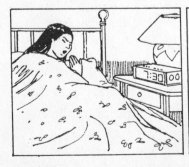

Practice B

Work with a partner to write sentences using *sometimes* and *usually*. Write about things that you do often.

Example: *I **usually** get up before 7:30.*

■■■■■ **Read and Think**

Read the information on the paycheck stub carefully. Circle any items you don't understand and discuss them with a partner or with the teacher. Then answer the questions.

P	FABER ELECTRICAL REPAIRS, INC.		Social Security No.	Name			Pay Period		Pay Date
A			077-32-3345	Phoumy, Buonpho			ENDING 12/27/9X		12/31/9X
Y	Hours/Units	Rate	Earnings	Type	Deduction	Type	Deduction	Type	
S						18100 MEDC		20100 SVGS	
T									
A									
T									
E									
M									
E	This Pay	Gross Pay 350.00	Federal Income Tax 70.00	Social Security Tax 21.00	State Income Tax 3.00	Local Income Tax	SUI/SDI	Net Pay 218.00	
N									
T	YTD								

1. What is gross pay? What is Bounpho's gross pay?
2. What is net pay? What is Bounpho's net pay?
3. How much federal and state tax does Bounpho pay each week? What is that money used for?
4. What is the Social Security Tax? What happens to that money?
5. What are the advantages of having money for savings deducted from your paycheck?
6. Can Bounpho decide not to have money deducted from her paycheck?

In Your Community

Find out the information individually or in groups and share it with your class.

The federal government collects income tax. Sometimes state and local governments collect income tax too. State and local governments may also collect taxes on things you buy. Bring in old bills and receipts you have at home. In class, make a chart listing the name of each item, the price without tax, the amount of tax, and the total cost with tax. Be sure to include bills or receipts for some of the following:

Household utilities (telephone, electricity, gas)
Meals in restaurants
Food purchased in a supermarket
Clothing
Cigarettes or liquor

■■■■■ Figuring Out the U.S.

As you read the passage and study the charts, circle any words you don't understand and try to guess their meanings.

The Federal Government Dollar

Where It Comes From		Where It Goes	
Individual Income Taxes	$.38	Social Security, Medicare, etc.	$.43
Social Security Taxes	$.32	National Defense	$.27
Borrowing	$.12	Interest on Loans	$.14
Corporate Income Taxes	$.11	Grants to State & Local Govt.	$.11
Other	$.07	Other	$.05

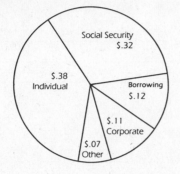

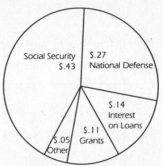

Estimates for fiscal year 1988–89

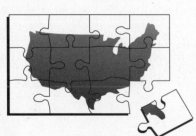

Most of the money required to operate the federal government comes from income and Social Security taxes paid by workers and employers. These taxes amount to over 80 percent of the total figure. You pay income tax based on how much you earn, and your employer pays taxes based on how much money the company makes. There is a difference, however. The company can sometimes make up for high taxes by charging customers higher prices.

The federal government borrows money to keep going. The first chart shows that 12 percent of the money it gets is borrowed money. The second chart shows that 14 percent of the money it spends is for interest on all those loans. How does this compare to your own personal budget?

Your Turn

Discuss the questions.

1. How much of each government dollar comes from Social Security taxes? from corporate taxes?
2. How much is spent on loans? on national defense?
3. What do you think about how the U.S. federal government gets and spends its money? Do you think any changes should be made?
4. What services does the U.S. federal government supply to you and your family? What are you paying for now that will benefit you in later years?

> *Choose one of the questions and write about it.*

Person A

Part 1

The pictures below show someone robbing a house. Describe the robbery to your partner and answer questions about what happened. You could start with these lines:

Person A: Last night someone broke into the house across the street.

Person B: That's terrible. How did you find out?

Part 2

After you have described the robbery and answered Person B's questions, your partner will describe a mugging pictured on his or her page. As you listen to the description, ask questions about the pictures on your partner's page. You can begin with some of the following.

1. How many people were there?
2. What did they look like?
3. What were they wearing?
4. What happened first? Then what?
5. What other details can you give?

Person B

Part 1

Your partner will describe a robbery pictured on his or her page. As you listen to the description, ask questions about the robbery. You can begin with some of the following.

1. How many people were there?
2. What did they look like?
3. What were they wearing?
4. What happened first? Then what?
5. What other details can you give?

Part 2

After you have finished asking your partner questions, it is your turn to describe a crime and answer some questions about it. The pictures below show someone being mugged. Describe the mugging and answer your partner's questions. You could start with these lines:

Person B: Yesterday, I saw someone get mugged in the park.

Person A: Oh, no! What happened?

My Papers Are Good

Before You Listen

1. Who are the two people? Where are they?
2. What is one man showing the other man?
3. What do you think they are talking about?
4. What do you know about employment rules in the United States?

▪▪▪▪▪ My Papers Are Good

Listen carefully to the dialogue.

Tony: So Fernando told you I'm looking for someone to repair televisions.

Gabriel: Yes, he did. I studied electronics at a technical school in Mexico. And I've been a television repairman for the last five years.

Tony: Where have you worked?

Gabriel: I worked at Mitchell Electric on Albion and Main. But they went out of business three weeks ago. I'm a hard worker, and I want to get back to work.

Tony: How long have you lived in the U.S.?

Gabriel: Since 1981.

Tony: Are you a U.S. citizen?

Gabriel: No. I'm a permanent resident. Look. Here's my I-688 EXT with the black sticker on the back.

Tony: I haven't seen one of those before. Don't you have a green card?

Gabriel: No, but my papers are good. I'm sure of it. Mr. Mitchell said they were all I needed. And he never did anything risky.

Tony: Well, thank you very much for coming in. I'll be talking with several other candidates. I'll call you in a few days.

Gabriel: OK, but . . .

Words to Know

repair	technical school	papers
electronics	sticker	candidates

_____   _____   _____

Another Way to Say It

on Albion and Main .... on the corner of Albion Street and Main Street

went out of business .... closed the company

_____ .... _____

■ ■ ■ ■ ■ Talking It Over

Discuss the questions in pairs or in groups.

1. What kind of work is Tony hiring someone to do?
2. What education and work experience does Gabriel have?
3. Why did Gabriel leave his last job?
4. What kind of employees do you think Tony wants to hire? (citizens? permanent residents? temporary residents?) Why do you think this?
5. Do you think Tony understands that Gabriel's papers are legal? What do you think Tony is afraid of?
6. Do you think Gabriel will get the job? Why or why not?
7. Have you heard of anyone in Gabriel's situation? What is he or she doing about it?
8. Do you have employment laws like this in your native country? How do they affect people there?

Working Together

When you look for a job, you will be asked about your education, what work you have done before, and what kind of working papers you have. With a partner, role-play applying for a job. Here is a sample opening:

Mr. Faber: What kind of education do you have?

You: I finished high school in Mexico.

Real Talk

We pronounce the plural *s* three different ways in English. It can sound like "s" in *residents*, "z" in *televisions*, or "iz" in *chances*. Listen and repeat as your teacher reads the following examples. Then write down other words with the plural *s*. Say them out loud and add them to the appropriate list.

"s"	"z"	"iz"
candidates	years	businesses
weeks	papers	licenses
_____	_____	_____

Using *In*, *On*, and *At* with Places

In is used before the names of cities, states, and countries.

How long have you lived **in** the U.S.?

On is used with street names.

Mitchell Electric is **on** Main Street.

At is used with organizations like schools and businesses.

I studied electronics **at** a technical school in Mexico.

Practice A

Raymond is at a job interview. Fill in the blanks using *in*, *on*, or *at*.

Pilár: And where did you study accounting?

Raymond: _____ Santa Rosa College.

Pilár: Oh. Which campus?

Raymond: The one _____ Airport Road _____ Union City.

Pilár: How long have you been _____ California?

Raymond: About four years. We stayed _____ the Pines Motel for a

month. Now we live _____ Church Street _____ the town of
Upland.

Pilár: Could you commute to Union City every day?

Raymond: Sure! I could park in the municipal lot _____ Summit Street.

Practice B

Work with a partner. Prepare some job interview questions asking where your
partner went to school, where he or she has worked, where he or she used to
live, and where he or she lives now. Your partner will prepare questions for
you. Then ask each other the questions. Pay attention to the use of *in*, *on*,
and *at*.

■■■■■ Read and Think

Read the following passage and try to guess the meanings of any words you don't know. Then answer the questions.

Know Your Rights

The Immigration Reform and Control Act of 1986—
- gives many undocumented immigrants a way of becoming legal permanent residents
- makes it illegal for an employer to discriminate against a legal immigrant in favor of a U.S. citizen

You cannot be refused a job just because—
- you were born in another country or you speak with an accent
- the employer isn't sure if your working papers are legal
- the employer wants to hire only U.S. citizens, instead of finding the best person for the job

If you think you are the victim of job discrimination—
- call the U.S. Department of Justice at 1-800-255-7688
- contact the local chapter of the American Civil Liberties Union
- visit your local Equal Employment Opportunity Commission office

---

1. How did the Immigration Reform and Control Act (the "amnesty" program) help some immigrants?
2. Do you know people who took advantage of the amnesty program? How did it help them?
3. What are the reasons some employers give for not hiring immigrants? Are these reasons legal?
4. Do you know anyone who has been the victim of job discrimination? What did the person do about it? What was the outcome?

In Your Community

Find out the information individually or in groups and share it with your class.

What agencies are there in your community that will help immigrants with job discrimination problems? Ask friends, religious leaders, and the reference librarian at the local public library for names and telephone numbers.

Then call or visit each agency to find out exactly what it can do to help. Later, work together to make a list of everything you found out. Make copies of the list to give to friends and relatives.

■ ■ ■ ■ ■ Figuring Out the U.S.

As you read the passage, circle any words you don't understand and try to guess their meanings.

Some Laws Against Discrimination

In the 1960s, the government passed many laws to fight different kinds of discrimination. Job discrimination was one problem. Often, employers refused to hire black workers. They sometimes hired white workers who were less qualified. The 1964 Civil Rights Act was passed to stop this practice. This law prohibits discrimination based on race, color, religion, sex, and national origin.

Before the 1960s, black people were prevented from voting in some places. The 1965 Voting Rights Act says that no U.S. citizen can be stopped from voting on the basis of race, color, religion, or national origin. An addition to this law says that voting materials should be translated into languages other than English. This makes it easier for immigrant citizens to vote.

Laws against discrimination have made it possible for some black people and other minorities to get better jobs, education, and housing. However, some people dislike these laws. For example, they think that less qualified minority workers get preference over whites. Other people feel these laws are a fair remedy for many years of unfair treatment.

Your Turn

Discuss the questions.

1. Which law made it easier for someone who reads little English to vote?
2. Which law made job discrimination illegal?
3. Do these laws protect black people only?
4. Do you think laws like these can stop discrimination? Why or why not?
5. Do you think these laws discriminate against whites? Why do you think some people have that opinion?
6. Who are "minorities" in the U.S.? Are there minority groups in your native country? Who are they?
7. Have you experienced discrimination? Where? What did you do? Could you have done anything else?

> *Choose one of the questions and write about it.*

I Want to Bring My Son Here

Before You Listen

1. What is Ms. Carey's job? How do you know?
2. What do you think the two women are talking about?
3. What do you know about immigration law?
4. Have you brought family members to live in the U.S.?

■■■■■ I Want to Bring My Son Here

Listen carefully to the dialogue.

Maria: I'm a permanent resident, and I want to bring my son here to live with me. Right now, he lives in Mexico with his grandmother.

Rita: Well, first you'll need to file a petition with the INS. It asks for information about your immigration status. You will also need a document that proves that the person you want to bring to the U.S. is really your son.

Maria: What can I show?

Rita: A copy of your son's birth certificate will do.

Maria: I suppose I should have it translated into English.

Rita: Right. Then you send in the petition, along with a copy of your green card and $75.

Maria: This isn't as complicated as I thought. When will my son get his permit to live in the U.S.?

Rita: The INS should approve the petition soon. But it may take as long as seven years to get an appointment at the U.S. consulate in Mexico.

Maria: Seven years!

Rita: The wait may get shorter, but that's what it looks like right now.

Maria: I can't believe it. By the time my son gets here, he'll be an adult.

Words to Know

permanent resident	complicated	appointment
petition	permit	consulate
birth certificate	approve	_____
_____	_____	

Another Way to Say It

A copy . . . will do. .... A copy . . . is enough proof.

I suppose .... I guess

_____ .... _____

Discuss the questions in pairs or in groups.

1. What kind of help is Maria looking for?
2. What steps will she have to follow?
3. What document will she need to show?
4. When will Maria's son be able to come to the U.S. to live?
5. Why do you think the process takes so long?
6. Do you think Maria will have to pay Rita? Why or why not?
7. Do you know anyone who has filed a petition to have a family member enter the country? Did that person get help with the process? How much did it cost?

Working Together

Before discussing bringing a family member to live in the U.S., people should understand something about the process and know what documents they will need. Work with a partner. Write out the basic steps in this process. Then list the documents you and your relative could use to meet each of the requirements.

Real Talk

When a word ends in *-tion*, the syllable just before the *-tion* is stressed (pronounced louder than the others). Listen as your teacher reads these examples from this lesson:

information   petition
immigration

Make a list of more *-tion* words with the teacher. Practice repeating the words after the teacher.

■ ■ ■ ■ ■ **Putting It Together**

Not as . . . as and Less . . . than
Here are two ways to make comparisons using *as* and *than*. Both
sentences mean the same thing.
     This **isn't as complicated as** I thought.
     This is **less complicated than** I thought.

Practice A

Change the *not as . . . as* sentences to *less . . . than* sentences. Change the
less . . . than sentences to *not as . . . as* sentences.

1. Bringing a relative to live in the U.S. is *less easy than* I thought.

   Bringing a relative to live in the U.S. is not as easy as I thought.

2. The fact sheet was *less helpful than* the lawyer.

   _____.

3. Where you're working is*n't as important as* your immigration status.

   _____.

4. The forms are*n't as confusing as* I thought they would be.

   _____.

5. Getting a driver's license was *less difficult than* bringing a relative to
   the U.S.

   _____.

Practice B

Work with a partner. Make up sentences like those above using *not as . . . as*
and *less . . . than*. You can get ideas from the picture.

   Example: *Gabriel thinks baseball is **less interesting than** soccer.*

Try using some of these words:
         difficult   interesting   exciting
         useful   expensive   dangerous

Read the following passage and try to guess the meanings of the underlined words. Then answer the questions.

Rights and Responsibilities

Everyone living in the United States has a <u>guarantee</u> of certain rights, <u>regardless</u> of his or her legal status.

- Everyone has the right to legal <u>counsel</u> if he or she is arrested.
- Everyone has the right to free speech.
- Everyone has the right to police <u>protection</u>.
- All children can attend a local <u>public</u> school for free.
- Emergency medical care is available to everyone through public hospitals.

Legal immigrants receive a variety of benefits, and they must follow certain rules. With a tourist visa, you are allowed to stay for a <u>limited</u> amount of time and are not allowed to work. With a student visa, you may stay while you are <u>enrolled</u> in school, and you may be allowed to work a limited number of hours in certain jobs.

A permanent resident can work in any available job and can leave and reenter the U.S. at any time. However, a permanent resident can lose this status and be <u>deported</u> if <u>convicted</u> of a serious crime. A citizen has the right to vote and to run for office. Citizens cannot be deported.

There are many agencies offering help to immigrants. These include legal aid societies, county boards of social services, and public law clinics.

1. What basic rights are guaranteed to everyone in the U.S.?
2. What benefits and regulations apply to people with tourist visas? with student visas?
3. What rights does a permanent resident have? a citizen?
4. Which agencies can help you get the benefits available to you?
5. Do you know anyone who has received help from an agency since arriving in the U.S.? What agency? What kind of help?

In Your Community

Find out the information individually or in groups and share it with your class.

Find out what kind of legal assistance is available in your community from legal aid societies, religious organizations, lawyers, and other groups. Start by asking friends and checking the local newspaper and the yellow pages of the phone book. Ask what help each agency is willing to give to undocumented immigrants, immigrants covered by the 1986 amnesty program, refugees, people seeking political asylum, and permanent residents.

■ ■ ■ ■ ■ Figuring Out the U.S.

As you read the advertisement, circle any words you don't understand and try to guess their meanings.

IMMIGRATION PROBLEMS?
We Guarantee Results!
Temporary Visas • Green Cards
Deportation Matters
First Visit Free!
Herbert F. Tager
Notary Public
Call 555-3552

It's Never Too Late—Call Us Now!

Your Turn

Discuss the questions.

1. Who do you think would respond to this advertisement? Why?
2. Would you trust Herbert F. Tager completely? Why or why not? How could you find out if he was reputable?
3. What problems can result from getting immigration advice from a disreputable person?
4. What does a notary public do? What does a lawyer do? How are the two jobs different?

> *Choose one of the questions and write about it.*

Before You Listen

1. What do you think Luz and Levent are talking about?
2. Have you ever looked at a book like the one on the table? What was in it? What did you think of it?
3. How does Luz feel about what she's saying? How do you know?
4. How does Levent feel about what Luz is saying?

■ ■ ■ ■ ■ But I Love My Native Country

Listen carefully to the dialogue.

Luz: Why can't you make up your mind about becoming a U.S. citizen?

Levent: All the benefits sound great, but I'm worried about what I'd have to leave behind.

Luz: Like what?

Levent: Well, if I make the U.S. my home for the rest of my life, I'll miss my family and my old friends.

Luz: Yes, but having a U.S. passport will make it easier for you to visit them whenever you want. And it's easier for citizens to bring close relatives here to live.

Levent: That's true. But I love my native country in a special way. I don't feel exactly the same about the U.S.

Luz: Of course not. But you won't stop loving your homeland just because you're making a new life here.

Levent: What about when I have children? They won't feel the same way about Turkey that I do.

Luz: That's true. But you can keep your customs and religion alive. And think of the advantages you'll be giving them—education, career opportunities, political freedom.

Levent: I understand. But I need to think it over.

Words to Know

benefits	homeland	opportunities
miss	customs	_____
close relatives	religion	_____

Another Way to Say It

make up your mind .... decide
Like what? .... Can you give me an example?
think it over .... think about it carefully
_____   ....   _____

■ ■ ■ ■ ■ Talking It Over

Discuss the questions in pairs or in groups.

1. What does Levent think he will miss if he becomes a U.S. citizen?
2. What solutions does Luz offer to this problem?
3. How does Levent feel about his native country? about the U.S.? Why doesn't he feel the same about both places?
4. What future problems does Levent expect if he becomes a citizen? Do these problems seem real to you? Why or why not?
5. Do you know anyone who feels the way Levent does? What other reasons does that person give for not wanting to become a U.S. citizen?
6. What advantages of U.S. citizenship does Luz talk about?
7. In addition to the reasons Luz gives, what advantages of U.S. citizenship do you know about?
8. Do you think every immigrant should become a U.S. citizen? Why or why not?

Working Together

Work with a partner to finish this conversation. Person A thinks all immigrants should try to become U.S. citizens. Person B disagrees.

Person A: When are you going to apply for citizenship?

Person B: I'm not sure I'm going to do that.

Real Talk

When you pronounce the *v* sound, your upper teeth should touch your lower lip. Listen to your teacher read the following words with the *v* sound. Then try pronouncing the words yourself.

visit   native
whenever   live

Now go back to the dialogue on page 74 and find other words with *v* to pronounce.

> **If Clauses**
>
> When you talk about the results of something that may (or may not) happen, use an *if* clause with a present-tense verb, followed by a main clause with a future-tense verb.
>
> *If* Clause   Main Clause
>
> If I **make** my home in the U.S., **I'll miss** my old friends.

Practice A

Complete the following sentences using present-tense verbs in each *if* clause and future-tense verbs in each main clause.

1. become a U.S. citizen/get a U.S. passport

   If Levent <u>becomes a U.S. citizen</u>, he<u>'ll get a U.S. passport</u>.

2. have a U.S. passport/be able to travel freely

   If he _____, he _____.

3. visit his native country/go see his old friends

   If he _____, he _____.

4. stay in the U.S./have many career opportunities

   If he _____, he _____.

5. become a U.S. citizen/not stop loving his homeland

   If Levent _____, he _____.

Practice B

Talk with a partner about some of your plans for the future and the possible results. Use an *if* clause followed by a main clause. Then write down some of your plans.

Example: *If I become a citizen, I'll bring my brother here to live.*

■ ■ ■ ■ ■ Read and Think

Read the flier and try to guess the meanings of the underlined words.
Then answer the questions.

Who Can Apply for U.S. Citizenship?

● You must be at least 18 years old.

● You must be a legal permanent resident.

● You must have lived in the U.S. as a legal permanent resident for at least five years (or have been married to a U.S. citizen for three years).

● You must have lived in the state where you are <u>filing</u> your <u>petition</u> for at least three months.

● You must be able to read, write, and understand simple English and know something about the history and government of the United States.

How to Apply for U.S. Citizenship

● Write to or visit your local Immigration and Naturalization Service (INS) office and request an "Application to File Petition for Naturalization."

● Fill out the application (Form N-400).
—Write your name exactly the same throughout.
—List <u>arrests</u>, even if for a <u>traffic ticket</u>.
—List membership in clubs and other organizations.

● Fill out the <u>Biographic</u> Information sheet (Form G325).

● Obtain a complete <u>fingerprint chart</u>.

---

1. Who is eligible to apply for U.S. citizenship?
2. What is the first step in getting an application?
3. What is a fingerprint chart, and why do you have to have one?
4. Do you know how a person becomes a citizen of your native country? How is it different from becoming a citizen of the U.S.?

In Your Community

Form three groups. One group will locate someone in the community who has recently become a citizen and invite that person to speak to the class and answer questions. Another group will visit or write to the nearest INS office and request citizenship application materials. The third group will find a representative of an immigrants' aid society who is willing to speak to the class.

Before the class visits, review the application forms and list any questions you may have for the speaker.

■■■■■ Figuring Out the U.S.

As you read the passage, circle any words you don't understand and try to guess their meanings.

Responsibilities of Citizens

Every citizen shares the responsibility to help make life better for everyone living in the United States. President John F. Kennedy summed up this idea when he said, ". . . ask not what your country can do for you; ask what you can do for your country."

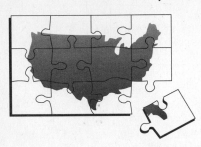

All citizens are expected to

Obey the law. City, state, and federal laws were created to protect the rights of all citizens.

Stay informed. By reading the newspaper, watching television, and talking with friends, citizens learn about the changes taking place in the country. They can then decide what action to take on important issues.

Vote. Each vote helps decide the future of the country.

Pay taxes. Citizens support the government, which supplies them with a wide variety of services and benefits.

Serve on a jury. Citizens are required to serve on a jury when summoned.

Defend the country. Citizens may be asked or required to serve in the armed forces.

Your Turn

Discuss the questions.

1. Repeat in your own words what President Kennedy said about the responsibilities of citizens. Do you agree?
2. What are some ways of becoming well informed? Why is it important for all citizens to be well informed?
3. Which responsibilities of citizenship do some people find difficult? Why do they feel this way?
4. How are the responsibilities of a citizen in the U.S. different from those in your native country? In what ways are they the same?

> *Choose one of the questions and write about it.*

Person A

Work with a partner. One of you should look only at this page, and the other should look only at page 80. Take turns asking each other for a definition of each word that is not filled in on your puzzle. At the end, go over all answers with your partner.

The first answer is written in for you. All answers are from Chapters 10–12. Some are two or more words long.

> Example: Person A: What is number 1 down?
>
> Person B: It's two words. It's the paper that every child needs.
>
> Person A: I can't guess. Can you try another definition?
>
> Person B: It's the paper you get when you are born.

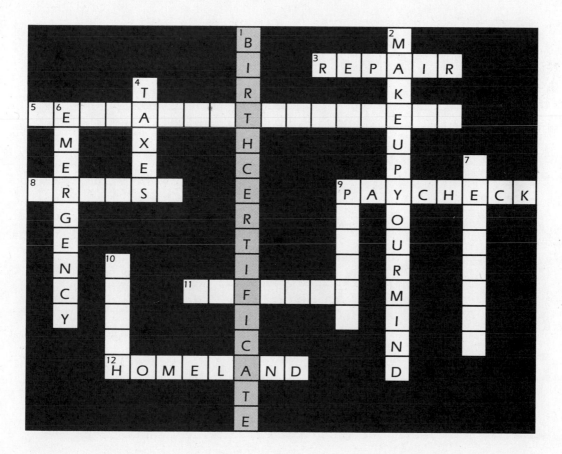

■ ■ ■ ■ ■ **Review Unit Four**

Person B

Work with a partner. One of you should look only at this page, and the other should look only at page 79. Take turns asking each other for a definition of each word that is not filled in on your puzzle. At the end, go over all answers with your partner.

The first answer is written in for you. All answers are from Chapters 10–12. Some are two or more words long.

Example: Person A: What is number 1 down?

Person B: It's two words. It's the paper that every child needs.

Person A: I can't guess. Can you try another definition?

Person B: It's the paper you get when you are born.

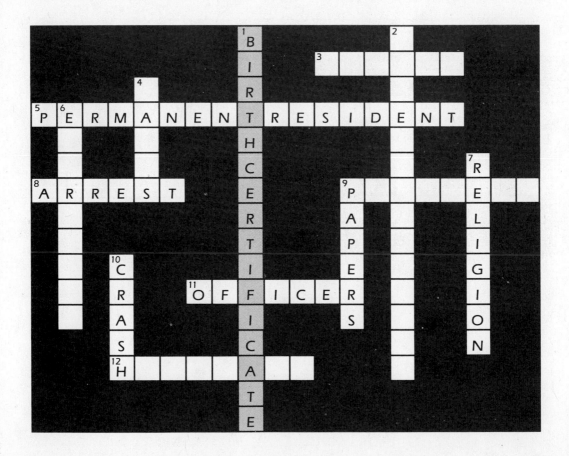

Appendix

Irregular Verbs in *It's Your Right*

Basic Form	Simple Past	Past Participle
break	broke	broken
bring	brought	brought
choose	chose	chosen
come	came	come
cost	cost	cost
do	did	done
drive	drove	driven
eat	ate	eaten
feel	felt	felt
fight	fought	fought
find	found	found
forget	forgot	forgotten
get	got	gotten
give	gave	given
go	went	gone
grow	grew	grown
have	had	had
hear	heard	heard
hit	hit	hit
hold	held	held
hurt	hurt	hurt
keep	kept	kept
know	knew	known
leave	left	left

Irregular Verbs in *It's Your Right* (continued)

Basic Form	Simple Past	Past Participle
make	made	made
pay	paid	paid
read	read	read
run	ran	run
say	said	said
see	saw	seen
send	sent	sent
show	showed	shown
speak	spoke	spoken
spend	spent	spent
stand	stood	stood
steal	stole	stolen
take	took	taken
teach	taught	taught
think	thought	thought
throw	threw	thrown
wear	wore	worn
write	wrote	written

■■■■■ Income Tax Return

Department of the Treasury - Internal Revenue Service

Form 1040EZ

Income Tax Return for
Single Filers With No Dependents (P)   199X

Name & address	Use IRS label (see page 9). If you don't have one, please print.

Print your name (first, initial, last)

Home address (number and street). (If you have a P.O. box, see page 9.)   Apt. no.

City, town or post office, state, and ZIP code. (If you have a foreign address, see page 9.)

Please print your numbers like this:

1234567890

Your social security number

Please see instructions on the back. Also, see the Form 1040EZ booklet.

Presidential Election Campaign (see page 9)
Do you want $1 to go to this fund?

Note: Checking "Yes" will not change your tax or reduce your refund. ▶

Yes No

Report your income

Attach Copy B of Form(s) W-2 here. Attach tax payment on top of Form(s) W-2.

Dollars   Cents

1   Total wages, salaries, and tips. This should be shown in Box 10 of your W-2 form(s). (Attach your W-2 form(s).)   **1**

2   Taxable interest income of $400 or less. If the total is more than $400, you cannot use Form 1040EZ.   **2**

3   Add line 1 and line 2. This is your **adjusted gross income.**   **3**

4   Can your parents (or someone else) claim you on their return?
☐ Yes. Do worksheet on back; enter amount from line E here.
☐ No. Enter 5,300.00. This is the total of your standard deduction and personal exemption.   **4**

Note: You must check Yes or No.

5   Subtract line 4 from line 3. If line 4 is larger than line 3, enter 0. This is your **taxable income.**   **5**

Figure your tax

6   Enter your Federal income tax withheld from Box 9 of your W-2 form(s).   **6**

7   **Tax.** Use the amount on **line 5** to find your tax in the tax table on pages 14–16 of the booklet. Enter the tax from the table on this line.   **7**

Refund or amount you owe

8   If line 6 is larger than line 7, subtract line 7 from line 6. This is your **refund.**   **8**

9   If line 7 is larger than line 6, subtract line 6 from line 7. This is the **amount you owe.** Attach your payment for full amount payable to "Internal Revenue Service." Write your name, address, social security number, daytime phone number, and "199X Form 1040EZ" on it.   **9**

Sign your return

Keep a copy of this form for your records.

I have read this return. Under penalties of perjury, I declare that to the best of my knowledge and belief, the return is true, correct, and complete.

Your signature   Date

X

For Privacy Act and Paperwork Reduction Act Notice, see page 4 in the booklet.   Form 1040EZ (199X)

199X Form W-4

Department of the Treasury
Internal Revenue Service

Purpose. Complete Form W-4 so that your employer can withhold the correct amount of Federal income tax from your pay.

Exemption From Withholding. Read line 6 of the certificate below to see if you can claim exempt status. *If exempt, complete line 6; but do not complete lines 4 and 5.* No Federal income tax will be withheld from your pay. Your exemption is good for one year only. It expires February 15, 199X.

Basic Instructions. Employees who are not exempt should complete the Personal Allowances Worksheet. Additional worksheets are provided on page 2 for employees to adjust their withholding allowances based on itemized deductions, adjustments to income, or two-earner/two-job situations. Complete all worksheets that apply to your situation. The worksheets will help you figure the number of withholding allowances you are entitled to claim. However, you may claim fewer allowances than this.

Head of Household. Generally, you may claim head of household filing status on your tax return only if you are unmarried and pay more than 50% of the costs of keeping up a home for yourself and your dependent(s) or other qualifying individuals.

Nonwage Income. If you have a large amount of nonwage income, such as interest or dividends, you should consider making estimated tax payments using Form 1040-ES. Otherwise, you may find that you owe additional tax at the end of the year.

Two-Earner/Two-Jobs. If you have a working spouse or more than one job, figure the total number of allowances you are entitled to claim on all jobs using worksheets from only one Form W-4. This total should be divided among all jobs. Your withholding will usually be most accurate when all allowances are claimed on the W-4 filed for the highest paying job and zero allowances are claimed for the others.

Advance Earned Income Credit. If you are eligible for this credit, you can receive it added to your paycheck throughout the year. For details, get Form W-5 from your employer.

Check Your Withholding. After your W-4 takes effect, you can use **Pub. 919,** Is My Withholding Correct for 199X?, to see how the dollar amount you are having withheld compares to your estimated total annual tax. Call 1-800-829-3676 to order this publication. Check your local telephone directory for the IRS assistance number if you need further help.

Personal Allowances Worksheet   For 199X, the value of your personal exemption(s) is reduced if your income is over $100,000 ($150,000 if married filing jointly, $125,000 if head of household, or $75,000 if married filing separately). Get Pub. 919 for details.

A   Enter "1" for **yourself** if no one else can claim you as a dependent . . . . **A** _____

B   Enter "1" if: 1. You are single and have only one job; or
                    2. You are married, have only one job, and your spouse does not work; or   **B** _____
                    3. Your wages from a second job or your spouse's wages (or the total of both) are $1,000 or less.

C   Enter "1" for your **spouse**. But, you may choose to enter "0" if you are married and have either a working spouse or more than one job (this may help you avoid having too little tax withheld) . . . . **C** _____

D   Enter number of **dependents** (other than your spouse or yourself) whom you will claim on your tax return . . . . . . **D** _____

E   Enter "1" if you will file as **head of household** on your tax return (see conditions under "Head of Household," above) . . **E** _____

F   Enter "1" if you have at least $1,500 of **child or dependent care expenses** for which you plan to claim a credit . . . . **F** _____

G   Add lines A through F and enter total here . . . . ▶ **G** _____

For accuracy, do all worksheets that apply.
- If you plan to **itemize or claim adjustments to income** and want to reduce your withholding, see the Deductions and Adjustments Worksheet on page 2.
- If you are **single** and have **more than one job** and your combined earnings from all jobs exceed $27,000 OR if you are **married** and have a **working spouse or more than one job,** and the combined earnings from all jobs exceed $46,000, see the Two-Earner/Two-Job Worksheet on page 2 if you want to avoid having too little tax withheld.
- If **neither** of the above situations applies, **stop here** and enter the number from line G on line 4 of Form W-4 below.

-------- **Cut here and give the certificate to your employer. Keep the top portion for your records.** --------

Form **W-4**
Department of the Treasury
Internal Revenue Service

Employee's Withholding Allowance Certificate
▶ **For Privacy Act and Paperwork Reduction Act Notice, see reverse.**

OMB No. 1545-0010
199X

1 Type or print your first name and middle initial	Last name	2 Your social security number

Home address (number and street or rural route)	3 Marital status	☐ Single ☐ Married
City or town, state, and ZIP code		☐ Married, but withhold at higher Single rate.

Note: *If married, but legally separated, or spouse is a nonresident alien, check the Single box.*

4 Total number of allowances you are claiming (from line G above or from the Worksheets on back if they apply) . . .	**4**	
5 Additional amount, if any, you want deducted from each pay	**5** $	

6 I claim exemption from withholding and I certify that I meet **ALL** of the following conditions for exemption:
- Last year I had a right to a refund of **ALL** Federal income tax withheld because I had **NO** tax liability; **AND**
- This year I expect a refund of **ALL** Federal income tax withheld because I expect to have **NO** tax liability; **AND**
- This year if my income exceeds $550 and includes nonwage income, another person cannot claim me as a dependent.

If you meet all of the above conditions, enter the year effective and "EXEMPT" here . . . . . ▶ **6** 19____

7 Are you a full-time student? (**Note:** *Full-time students are not automatically exempt.*) . . . . **7** ☐ Yes ☐ No

Under penalties of perjury, I certify that I am entitled to the number of withholding allowances claimed on this certificate or entitled to claim exempt status.

Employee's signature ▶ _____   Date ▶ _____ , 19___

8 Employer's name and address (**Employer:** Complete 8 and 10 **only if** sending to IRS)	9 Office code (optional)	10 Employer identification number

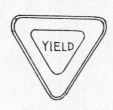

■■■■■ Index

The following is a list of the words and phrases found in the **Words to Know** *and* **Another Way to Say It** *sections.*